Other giftbooks by Helen Exley:
A Little Book for My Mother
Golf Quips
In Praise and Celebration of Daughters
The Best of Father Quotations

Published simultaneously in 1998 by Exley Publications Ltd
in Great Britain, and
Exley Publications LLC in the USA.

12 11 10 9 8 7 6 5 4 3 2 1

ISBN 1-86187-128-7

Edited and pictures selected by Helen Exley.
Picture research by Image Select International.
Printed in China.

**Exley Publications Ltd, 16 Chalk Hill, Watford, Herts
WD1 4BN, UK.
Exley Publications LLC, 232 Madison Avenue, Suite 1206,
NY 10016, USA.**

Thoughts on...
BEING A FATHER

A HELEN EXLEY GIFTBOOK

EXLEY
NEW YORK • WATFORD, UK

No man can possibly know

No man can possibly know
what life means, what the world
means, what anything means,
until he has a child and loves it.
And then the whole universe changes
and nothing will ever again
seem exactly as it seemed before.

LAFCADIO HEARN

A FATHER IS BORN

... [the baby's] shrivelled body and bent-up limbs, produced in me, even before I knew its sex, a jolting charge of love that was so powerful and intense I felt I had virtually been born again myself. There was no pause while I opened myself to feeling, no interval of gradually swelling emotion, just an instantaneous onslaught of grabbing, all-consuming love.

FRASER HARRISON, b.1944, FROM "A FATHER'S DIARY"

This moment of meeting seemed to be a birthtime for both of us; her first and my second life. Nothing, I knew, could ever be the same again, and I think I was reasonably shaken.

LAURIE LEE (1914-1997), FROM "TWO WOMEN"

BEAUTIFUL, BEAUTIFUL BABY

Proud parents that we were, we thought our daughter was perfect, from her shapely head to her pudgy toes.

BILLY GRAHAM

A baby overwhelms us with its lovableness; even its smell stirs us more deeply than the smell of pine or baking bread. What is overpowering is simply the fact that a baby is life. It is also a mess, but such an appealing one that we look past the mess to the jewel underneath.

BILL COSBY, b.1937, FROM *"FATHERHOOD"*

Women accost me.... "Isn't he lovely" they coo as he dozes in his Swedish papoose. "Looks just like his dad." I am in baby heaven.

CHRISTY CAMPBELL, FROM *"THE SUNDAY TELEGRAPH"*, 1996

THE FIRST-TIME FATHER

The first-time father, beside himself with excitement over the birth of his son, was determined to follow all the rules to a T. "So tell me, Nurse," he asked as his new family headed out the hospital door, "what time should we wake the little guy in the morning?"

AUTHOR UNKNOWN

When my wife became pregnant, the second thing I felt was a spontaneous gush of pleasure and pride, even though it was not planned, by me anyway, and I had not been consulted. The first thing was the thought – "I must tell her I am not up to wiping babies' bottoms."

ALAN BRIEN,
FROM "THE EXTENDED FLOWER", IN "FATHERHOOD"

Adieu long lie-ins on weekends.
Adieu grabbing a small bag and a passport,
and disappearing to Patagonia for a month.
Adieu travelling lightly through life.
Children demand your complete attention.
They become your foremost personal
and fiscal priority. They take over your life –
and, of course, you wouldn't want it
any other way.

DOUGLAS KENNEDY

Before i knew what love was

Before I met Stanley, I was the kind of person who, if I said "Sit" to a dog, it immediately had a hysterical fit, and if I tried to control a horse, it would throw me. I was useless with children, animals, and people. Relationships were things you got into by mistake, and love was a feeling I had if I really fancied someone a lot. Something happened, and I think it took about four seconds, when they handed me that screaming little blue bundle in the hospital birthing room. In that moment, I understood that love is an action, not a feeling, it's what you consciously decide to do.

NIGEL PLANER

A SURVIVAL COURSE!

Dad has to instantly absorb info on car seats, croup, origami, and oatmeal, stuff a man without kids simply does not have to master. Dad has to know how to get a tiny stretchy sock on a humid kid foot, how to get a giant frayed shoelace through a teensy little shoelace hole, and how to repair a doll's earring.

HUGH O'NEILL, FROM *"A MAN CALLED DADDY"*

Never assume something is childproof. A three-year-old could put Houdini to shame.

H. JACKSON BROWN JNR

THE FULL CATASTROPHE!

... fatherhood is a bridge, a passage from all those windy, heroic vows to the real-life elations of doing your best on behalf of the kids. Now I know that fatherhood is a pilgrim's path, littered with marbles and most of your plans.

HUGH O'NEILL, FROM *"A MAN CALLED DADDY"*

... before they could even walk or talk, my children have been determining where we live, where we eat, who we make friends with and how we spend our weekends.
Free time? Free will, even? For parents, there is no longer any such thing.

CHRISTOPHER MIDDLETON,
FROM *"WEEKEND TELEGRAPH"*, **1997**

CRAZY IN LOVE

A newborn baby is merely a small, noisy object, slightly fuzzy on one end, with no distinguishing marks to speak of.... But to its immediate family, it is without question the most phenomenal, the most astonishing, the most absolutely unparalleled thing that has yet occurred in the entire history of this planet.

IRVIN S. COBB

A baby, sells itself and needs no advertising copy; few people can resist it. There is something about babyness that brings out the softness in people and makes them want to hug and protect this small thing that moves and dribbles and produces what we poetically call poopoo. Even that becomes precious, for the arrival of a baby coincides with the departure of our minds.

BILL COSBY, b.1937, FROM "FATHERHOOD"

MY FRIEND

What I got was a friend – someone who needs and trusts me, someone I can go to football matches with, someone who smiles when I tickle him and cries if I go out in the car without him, a pal who rushes into my room every morning and pulls my glasses off my nose when I'm trying to read a paper. I got someone so dear to me that I cry tears of joy when I look at him asleep in his cot at night.

**UNKNOWN FATHER, FROM *"THE FIRST-TIME FATHER"*,
BY GRAHAM HART**

The great gift

When you are a father, and you hear your children's voices, you will feel that those little ones are akin to every drop in your veins; that they are the very flower of your life and you will cleave so closely to them that you seem to feel every movement that they make.

HONORÉ DE BALZAC (1799-1850), FROM "LE PÈRE GORIOT"

Of all nature's gifts to the human race, what is sweeter to a man than his children?

CICERO (106-43 B.C.)

EVERYTHING'S CHANGED

Since I have been a father, the pendulum of my
life swings through a wider arc. Before Josh
and Rebecca, I rarely whispered and I rarely
yelled. Now I do both all the time. Before Josh
and Rebecca, I merely strode through the world
like a man. Now I crawl, hunker, scramble, hop
on one foot, often see the world from my hands
and knees. Before Josh and Rebecca, I knew
nothing about water slides. Now I hold several
American records in the over-thirty-five
division. Before Josh and Rebecca, I heard only
the sound of my own voice. Now I sometimes
hear the principal, asking to see me at my
"earliest possible convenience." Now I always
carry two small voices in my soul. Before Josh
and Rebecca the world was plain. Now it's
fancy, full of portents and omens, solemnity
and awe.

HUGH O'NEILL, FROM *"A MAN CALLED DADDY"*

TIPS FOR POOR OLD DAD

The quickest way to get your children's attention is to sit down and look comfortable.

AUTHOR UNKNOWN

Never raise your hand to your children; it leaves your midsection unprotected.

ROBERT ORBEN

When you are dealing with a child, keep all your wits about you, and sit on the floor.

A. O'MALLEY

A new father quickly learns that his child comes to the bathroom at the wrong times. The only way for this father to be certain of bathroom privacy is to shave at the gas station.

BILL COSBY, b.1937, FROM "FATHERHOOD"

RUNNING RINGS AROUND DAD

You can learn many things from children. How much patience you have, for instance.

FRANKLIN P. JONES

They began borrowing things from me about the time they started to walk. They not only borrow in good family tradition, they're outright, no-return thieves. And now they've even taught my wife.

The only thing they haven't lifted is my toothbrush. The time I found my small daughter using it as a shoe dauber doesn't count. She "intended" to return it to the bathroom, she said.

The trouble is that... a hiding place good enough to baffle my thieves is usually good enough to baffle me. Indeed, I never have found the clothes-brush I hid after discovering (while brushing a blue flannel suit) that it had been used for grooming an Angora cat named Snow White....

P.C. BLACKBURN, FROM "THE BEAUTIFUL THIEVES IN MY GARDEN", "READER'S DIGEST", 1957

HOW CAN ONE SAY NO?

How can one say no to a child?
How can one be anything but a slave to
one's own flesh and blood?

HENRY MILLER (1891-1980)

There's no such thing as a little girl. As soon as
they come out of the womb, they're cut-down
women and they have all the wiles of women
from day one. They know how to manipulate
men. Daughters manipulate fathers and fathers
are quite happy for that to happen.

BARRY NORMAN

LIFE WILL NEVER BE THE SAME

Having a child alters the rights of every man, and I don't expect to live as I did without her. I am hers to be with, and hope to be what she needs, and know of no reason why I should ever desert her.

LAURIE LEE (1914-1997), FROM *"I CAN'T STAY LONG"*

Becoming a father changes everything. And I do mean everything; the way you speak, the way you work, sleep, drive, eat, dress, think. It even changes what you sing. Fatherhood changes your posture, your sex life, your hairstyle, your feelings about money, politics, God, about your past, and about the planet's future. Children change the ground you walk on.

HUGH O'NEILL, FROM *"A MAN CALLED DADDY"*

BEING WITH EACH OTHER

My daughters see me as an integral part of their lives. They can come to me in happiness and sadness. I am involved in their discipline as well as their creativity and fun. We are able to learn and share together.

GERALD M. TUCKMAN

Children have this amazing ability to bring out the child in you. It's the best feeling when you sit in the car and they start giggling or when you hear them saying to their dolls what you have said to them.

MIDGE URE

TOGETHER TIME

I'm there for... not just the bad stuff but the good as well – spontaneous hugs, unequivocal love, questions as he begins to make sense of the world ("Dada, what are cannonballs for?"), building sandcastles on the beach, first experiences of museums and zoos and food cooked in restaurants, the cinema and, best of all, sleepy cuddles in bed on mornings when neither of us can think of anything we'd rather do.

HUMPHREY PRICE,
FROM "HOME & LIFE", 1997

No music is so pleasant to my ears as that word – father. Zoroaster tells us that children are a bridge joining this earth to a heavenly paradise.... Blessed indeed is the man who hears many gentle voices call him father.

L. M. CHILD

Life's aspirations come in the guise of children.

RABINDRANATH TAGORE (1861-1941), FROM *"FIREFLIES"*

I have found the happiness of parenthood
greater than any other that I have experienced.

BERTRAND RUSSELL (1872-1970)

WITH MY WHOLE HEART

It is not so strange that I love you with my whole heart, for being a father is not a tie which can be ignored. Nature in her wisdom has attached the parent to the child and bound them spiritually together with a Herculean knot. This tie is the source of my consideration for your immature minds, a consideration which causes me to take you often into my arms. This tie is the reason why I used to dress you in silken garments and why I never could endure to hear you cry.

SIR THOMAS MORE (1478-1535)

... TO BE A GOOD PARENT

Marrying, founding a family, accepting all the children that come, supporting them in this insecure world and perhaps even guiding them a little, is I am convinced, the utmost a human being can succeed in doing at all.

FRANZ KAFKA (1883-1924)

The chances are that you will never be elected president of the country, write the great American novel, make a million dollars, stop pollution, end racial conflict, or save the world. However valid it may be to work at any of these goals, there is another one of higher priority – to be an effective parent.

LANDRUM BOLLING

Nothing I have ever done has given me
more joys and rewards than being a father
to my children.

BILL COSBY, b.1937, FROM "FATHERHOOD"

I'm a father. It's what I've always wanted to be.
It's what I almost always love doing. It is the
only thing in my life that day in and out makes
me feel like a good man. A real man. A man.
No need for applause. Lots of need for less
ridicule.

ART KLEIN

Having kids
is the most innately positive thing
that anyone can do.

**JACK NICHOLSON, b.1937,
FROM "*OK!*" MAGAZINE, 1997**

THE SAD TIMES

The saddest thing that every parent has
discovered since the days of the cave is that
some things cannot be taught.
Every single generation has to rediscover them
all on their own.
And the parents have to stand back and let
it happen.
And it hurts.

PETER DUGDALE

Every parent is at some time the father of the
unreturned prodigal, with nothing to do but
keep his house open to hope.

JOHN CIARDI

Reconnected to my feelings

I made a discovery late in life that astounds me to this day. It is very simple, basic, and powerful. I married late and had my first child at age thirty-five. That baby girl reconnected me to the very core of my feelings with such power and such ease, it was like being plugged into a socket after a lifetime of running on batteries. I'd find myself giggling and laughing at nothing more than her tiny hand curled around my finger.... At first, it was disorienting because suddenly all these feelings were sprouting up all over the place and I didn't always know how to react.... But gradually I learned that everything I felt was like a very simple and very pure message to myself. It may sound obvious, but for men especially it is a profound learning – the more attention I paid to how I was feeling, the more I liked myself and the more I found myself acting like the man I wanted to be.

THE EDITORS OF CONARI PRESS,
FROM *"THE PRACTICE OF KINDNESS"*

Until the day you die...

It's a frightening undertaking – becoming a parent. To be totally responsible for the development of a tiny human being is an intimidating proposition. It has been said that the greatest challenge to the human mind is a blank piece of paper. Not so. The greatest challenge is the blank slate of a newborn.

KEVIN KISHBAUGH

I think you worry about your children all the time. I had this idea that I'd worry about them until they were eighteen and went off to university. They would graduate and it would be great. That's nonsense. You worry about them more as they get older. You probably don't need to – it just happens. It's a parental thing. You worry about your children until the day you die.

BARRY NORMAN, FROM *"THE EXPRESS"*

ONLY LOVE

What I have learned in the process of raising
(four) daughters – and perhaps it applies to
other human affairs as well – is that there is no
single answer, no magic formula, no rigid set of
guidelines, no simple blueprint, no book of
easy instructions, no sure way of side-stepping
difficulties, no easy way out. There is love.

GEORGE LEONARD

Our children are not our own.... They are not
ours to keep but to rear.... They are not given to
us so that we can force them to fulfill our lives
and thus, in some way, cancel our failures.
They are not tools to be used, but souls to be
loved.

THOMAS C. SHORT

"WITHOUT THEM I AM NOTHING"

I love my three children more than anything in the world. I would do anything to protect them from harm. Without them I am nothing.
I cannot describe the feeling a father has for his children.

BOB GELDOF, b.1954,
FROM *"THE SUNDAY EXPRESS"*, 1996

It was Tilly who first roused in me the fiercest, deepest feeling of love I have ever experienced and to some extent Jack simply inherited these. Before she was born, I was unfulfilled, an emotionally smaller person. She brought about this new growth in me....

FRASER HARRISON, b.1944, FROM *"A FATHER'S DIARY"*

A CHILD'S LOVE

We made our way together to a big tree on the
lawn. He paused there. Then he took my hand
he was holding and pressed it to his cheek and

held it there. I thought at that instant I would
never feel unloved again.... There is a sense of
eternal comfort, but you can't express it, when
your heart is in another's hand.

ART KLEIN, FROM *"DAD AND SON"*

Acknowledgements: The publishers are grateful for permission to reproduce copyright material. Whilst every reasonable effort has been made to trace copyright holders, the publishers would be pleased to hear from any not here acknowledged. P.C. BLACKBURN: From *The Beautiful Thieves in My Garden*, from Reader's Digest, 1957. BILL COSBY: From *Fatherhood*, © 1986 William J. Cosby Jr. Published by Doubleday a division of Bantam Doubleday Dell Publishing Group. FRASER HARRISON: From *A Father's Diary*, © 1985 Fraser Harrison. Published by Fontana. Used with permission of the author. LEE IACOCCA: From *Talking Straight with Sonny Kleinfield*, © 1988 Lee Iacocca. Published by Bantam, a division of Bantam Doubleday Dell Publishing Group. DOUGLAS KENNEDY: From *Fatherhood in You* magazine, *Mail on Sunday*, March 1996. ART KLEIN: from *Dad and Son*, © Art Klein 1996. Published by Octavia Press. Used with permission of the author. LAURIE LEE: From I Can't Stay Long, published by Andre Deutsch, reprinted with permission of Penguin Books Ltd & Peters Fraser & Dunlop Group Ltd. HUGH O'NEILL: From *A Man Called Daddy*, © 1996 Hugh O'Neill. Reprinted by permission of Rutledge Hill Press, Nashville. NIGEL PLANER: From *A Good Enough Dad*, © 1992 Nigel Planer. Published by Arrow Books. HUMPHREY PRICE: From *Me and Fred*, from *Home and Life*, June 1997.

Picture credits: Exley Publications would like to thank the following organizations and individuals for permission to reproduce their pictures. Whilst every reasonable effort has been made to trace the copyright holders, the publishers would be pleased to hear from any not here acknowledged. Alinari (A), Archiv Für Kunst (AKG), Art Resource (AR), Bridgeman Art Library (BAL), Christie's Images (CI), Gamma, Giraudon (GIR), Scala (SCA), Statens Konstmuseer (SKM); SuperStock (SS), The Image Bank (TIB). Cover: © 1998 Patti Mollica, *Father and Kids*, SS; title-page: Wilhelm Rudolph, *The Family*, AKG; p7: © 1998 Patti Mollica, *Father and Kids*, SS; p9: © 1998 William Frederick Elwell, *The First Born*, BAL; p10: T. Gaponenko, *Feeding Time*, , SCA; p12: © 1998 William H. Johnson, *A Young Pastry Cook*, AKG; p15: Alvar Jansson, *Sondagskladd familj*, (SKM); p17: Leonid Ossipovitch Pasternak, *Evening Before the Examination*, AR; p18: © 1998 Robert Medley, *The Butcher's Shop*, BAL; p20: Theodore Thomas; p22: © 1998 Maxwell Ashby Armfield, *Portrait of Keith Henderson in a Black Hood*, BAL; p24: Wilhelm Rudolph, *The Family*, AKG; p26: © 1998 Ellis Wilson, *Field Workers*, National Museum of American Art, Washington DC/AR; p29: Marcucci Mario, *Self-portrait*, SCA; p31: © 1998 Christian Pierre, *Dream Book*, SS; p32: © 1998 Bonnie Timmons, *Familial Fatness*, TIB; p34: Arthur Hughes, *Lost Child*, CI; p36: © 1998 Karen Armitage, *Lynford*, 1969, BAL; p38: © 1998 Hartmut Genz, *A Visiting Performance of the Soviet State Circus in East Germany*, AKG; p40: © 1998 Christian Pierre, *Modern Madonna*, SS; pp42/43: Claude Monet, *Rising Sun*, Gamma; p44: Veronese (1528-1588), *Ritratto del conte da Porto con il figlio Adriano*, SCA; p46: © 1998 Glyn Warren Philpot, *Felix*, BAL; p49: © 1998 Adolf Wissel, *Peasant Family of Kalenberg*, Lauros-GIR; p50: Paul Gauguin & C Pissarro, *Portrait of Pissarro by Gauguin and Portrait of Gauguin by Pissarro*, GIR/BAL; p53: Francois Gerard, *The Painter Jean-Baptiste Isabey (1767-1855) and his daughter Alexandrine, child, later Mme Ciceri (1791-1871)*, GIR; p55: Arthur Evans, *Painting of Sir Arthur Evans*, Ashmolean Museum, Oxford; p56: Moricci Giuseppe, *Invito alla formazione della societa' di mutuo soc corso nel 1851*, SCA; p59: © 1998 Willi Balendat, *Fairground Onlookers*, AKG; pp60/61: Paul Gauguin & C Pissarro, *Portrait of Pissarro by Gauguin and Portrait of Gauguin by Pissarro*, GIR/BAL.